REPRODEPOT PATTERN BOOK: FLORA

REPRODEPOT PATTERN BOOK: FLORA

225 VINTAGE-INSPIRED TEXTILE DESIGNS

By Djerba Goldfinger

Foreword by Grace Bonney

Crafts by Mollie Green

CHRONICLE BOOKS

SAN FRANCISCO

Patterns copyright © 2009 by Djerba Goldfinger
Foreword copyright © 2009 by Grace Bonney
Project text copyright © 2009 by Mollie Green
Photographs copyright © Liz Daly

Library of Congress Cataloging-in-Publication Data available.

ISBN: 978-0-8118-6749-8

Manufactured in China
Designed by Also
Prop styling by Jenna Cushner and Le Petit Graphiste

10 9 8 7 6 5 4 3 2 1

Chronicle Books LLC
680 Second Street
San Francisco, California 94107

www.chroniclebooks.com

Illustrator is a registered trademark of Adobe Systems Incorporated.
Photoshop is a registered trademark of Adobe Systems Incorporated.
QuickBooks is a registered trademark of Intuit Inc.
X-Acto is a registered trademark of Elmer's Products, Inc.

TABLE OF CONTENTS

FOREWORD BY GRACE BONNEY 10
INTRODUCTION 12
TEXTILE PATTERNS 14
HOW TO USE THE DISK AND PATTERNS 240
PAPER CRAFTS 243

LICENSE AGREEMENT 264
THUMBNAIL INDEX 266

GRACE BONNEY Creator of Design*Sponge

In a world where everything from living-room sets to entire homes comes pre-fabricated, I find a shop such as Reprodepot a welcome reminder that not everyone is looking for a generic, prechosen style. As our society becomes increasingly focused on machine-made goods, a growing number of people have decided to return to the world of handmade, customizable design. And Djerba Goldfinger's Reprodepot makes such a world possible. By providing an astonishing range of beautiful fabrics, patterns, and crafting tools, Reprodepot plays an important role in the movement to reclaim our homes and make them our own.

Whether you're looking for the latest fabrics from Amy Butler or new Japanese imports, Djerba always seems to have them all—at prices to fit even the tightest budget. In the past, crafting options were limited to what you could find at your local art supply store; but these days it's as easy as opening your laptop to find fantastic textiles for home projects.

Every day I hear from DIY enthusiasts and design fans looking for inexpensive ways to decorate and furnish their homes. Whether they're looking to make their first quilt, create a decorative wall panel, or sew custom upholstery for a flea-market find, nothing is more popular right now than patterned fabric.

Choosing a bold print, an exotic weave, or a wood-grained pattern is a great way to bring color and energy into your home without a lot of effort or money. Crafters interested in patterns have always been able to get what they need at Reprodepot. Djerba's wide selection of patterned fabrics (arranged by style and time period) are the perfect solution for those looking to create projects with their own two hands.

No matter what type of textiles you're seeking, or what type of home project you're looking to complete, Djerba's incredible eye for color, print, and pattern set Reprodepot apart from other fabric purveyors. With this book, her love of pattern is fully realized and laid out for all of us to enjoy. There's something here for everyone, and I'm thrilled that Djerba has again provided us with a resource to inspire creativity and endless possibilities for handmade projects.

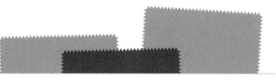

DJERBA GOLDFINGER Founder of Reprodepot Fabrics

I've always loved textiles—especially vintage textiles. From childhood, I've found the color combinations and sweet patterns in vintage fabrics irresistible. I started collecting vintage textiles and soon found that I had so many that there was no way I was ever going to use them all. This led me to start my business, Reprodepot Fabrics. Today, Reprodepot stocks both vintage-inspired textiles from fabulous designers and authentic vintage fabrics.

Ever since I started my business, I've wanted to make textile patterns available to crafters so they could use them in all sorts of projects. That's what you get in this handy book. You'll find 75 different designs—each in three different colors. You can flip through to pick your favorites and then pop the disk in to print them out on a color printer. You can also use them on your computer as wallpaper or for design accents.

At back we've included ten fun paper crafts to get your creative juices flowing. Because that's what this book is all about—inspiring creativity. Whether you're a beginning crafter or a seasoned expert, I hope you'll find lots of inspiration in the coordinated patterns provided within. From something so simple as a single sheet of stationery to write a thank-you note to a friend to a handmade one-of-a-kind journal, you will find that this book and disk will help you

create unique items with the pattern of your choosing. There are literally hundreds of possible combinations to be made with these designs. That's a lot of possibilities!

In the back of this book you'll find technical instructions on how to use the patterns, but I thought it'd be good to include some nontechnical instructions that may help you get the most out of this book.

#1: HAVE FUN!
Art should be fun. If it's not fun, keep trying until it is. It doesn't have to be taken so seriously.

#2: BE CREATIVE!
There is no right or wrong in art. Do what feels good to you and enjoy the creative process. You are an individual. What looks right to you may not look right to someone else. That's okay. In fact, it's even more than okay. Your particular vision is what will inspire you to continue creating and inspire others to find their creativity as well.

#3: DON'T WORRY!
You will make mistakes. Mistakes are great. Some of the world's greatest discoveries started out as a mistake. In fact, go ahead and deliberately try to make a mistake. See what happens. You may be surprised at how well it turns out!

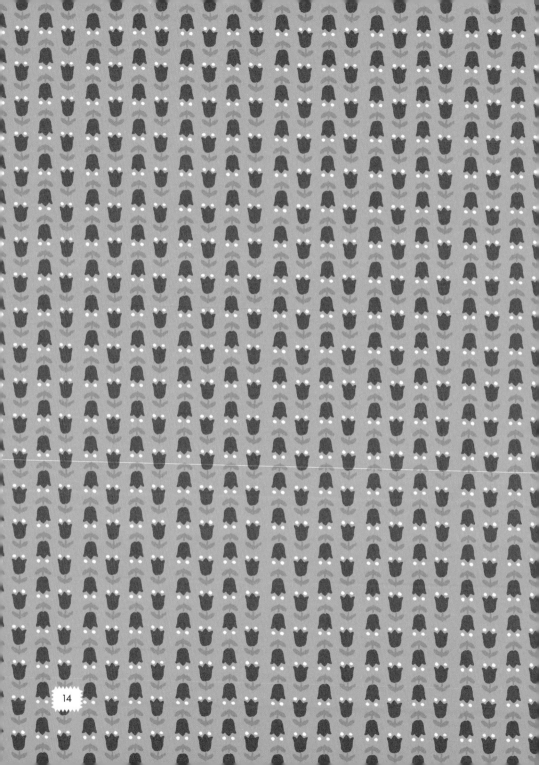

16

17

20

21

23

24

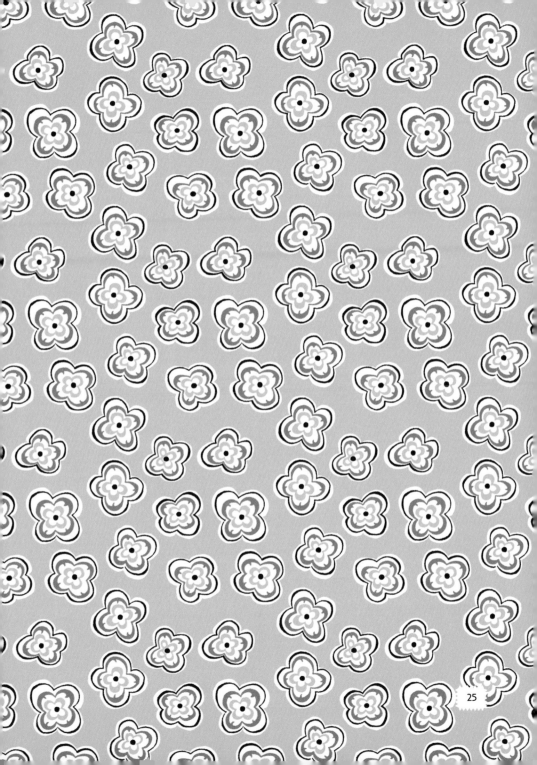

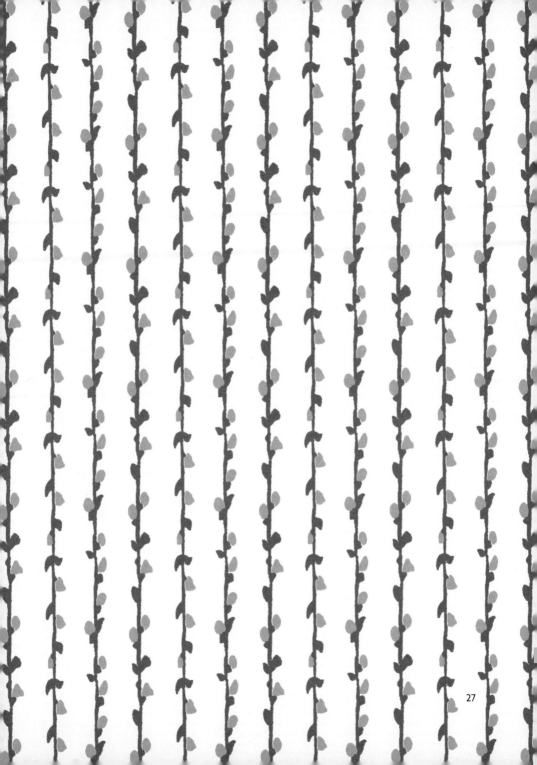

30

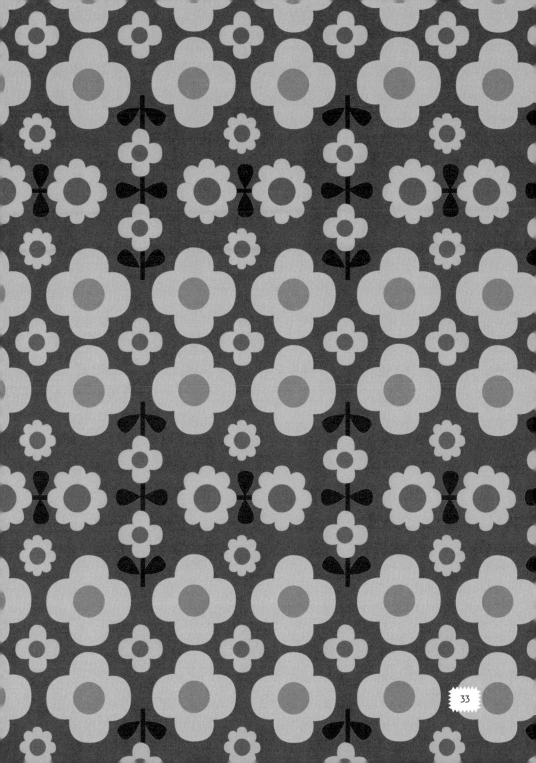

41

42

43

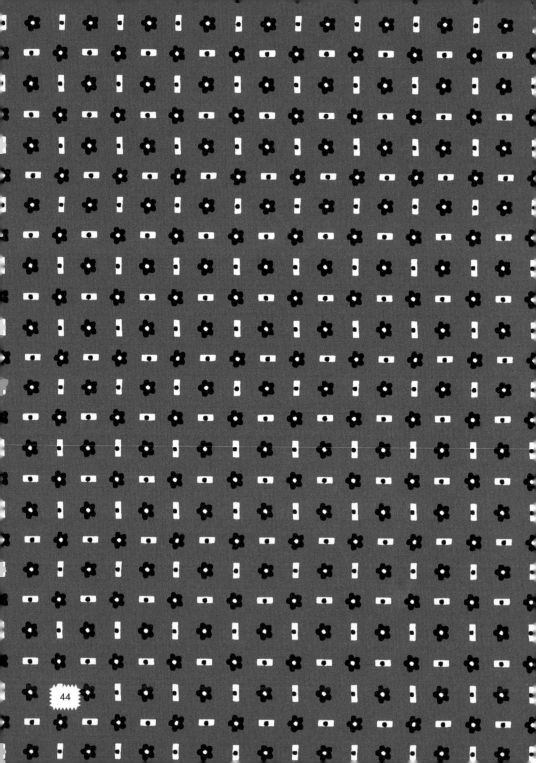

44

45

46

48

49

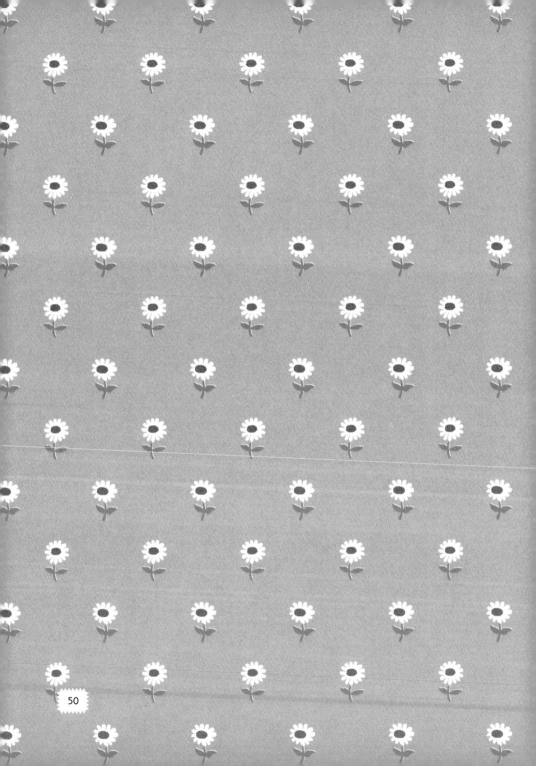

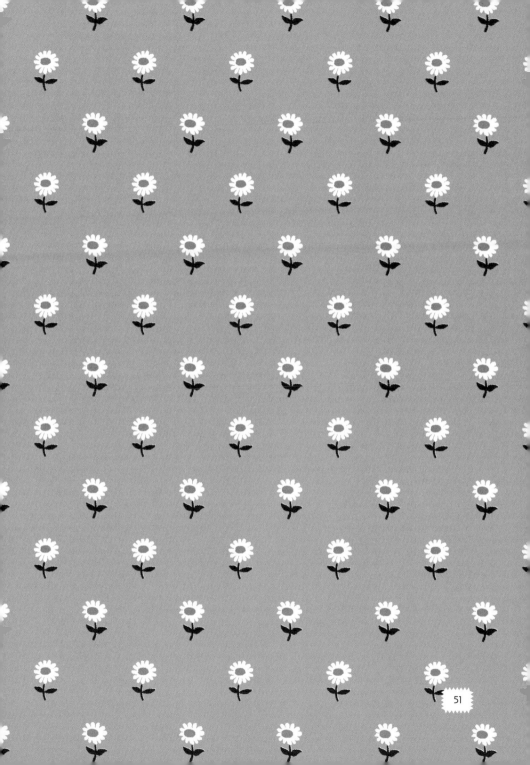

51

52

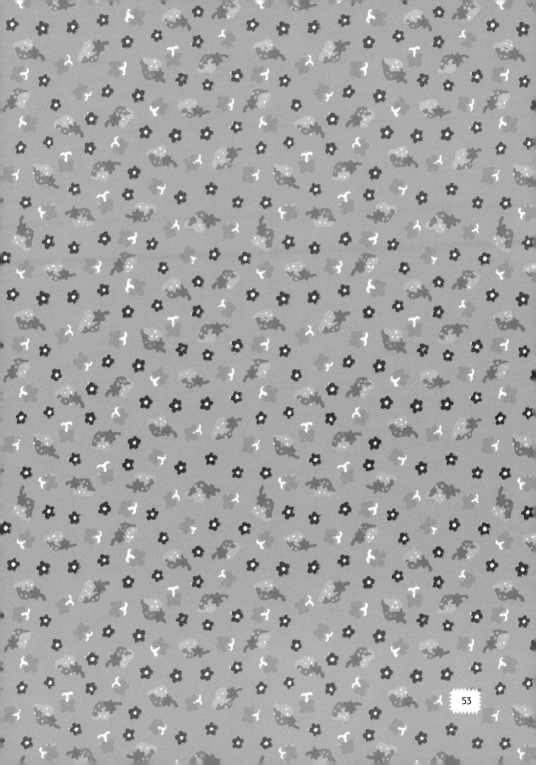

53

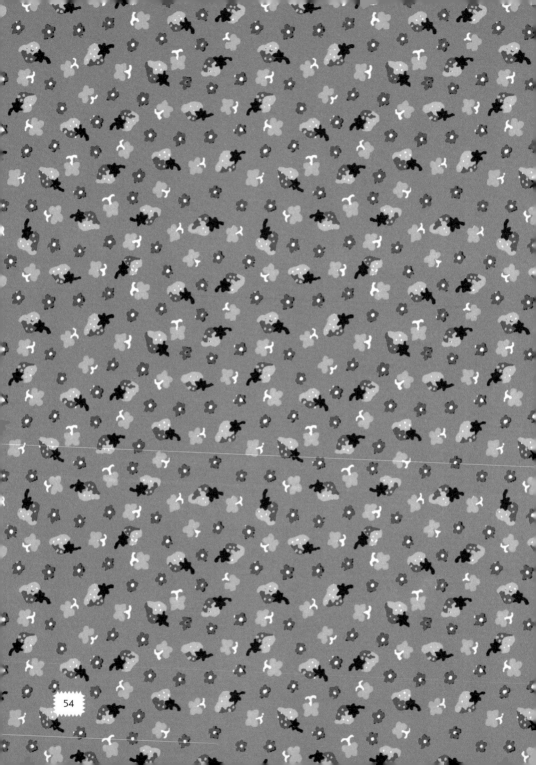

54

55

58

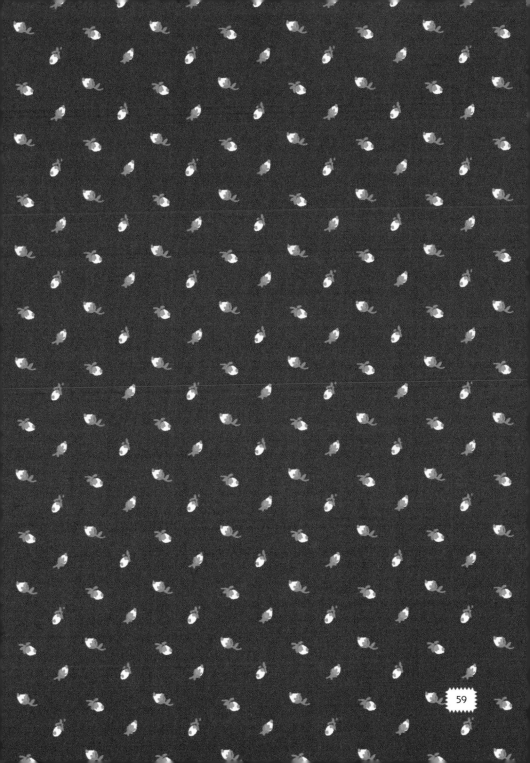

59

61

63

64

65

66

69

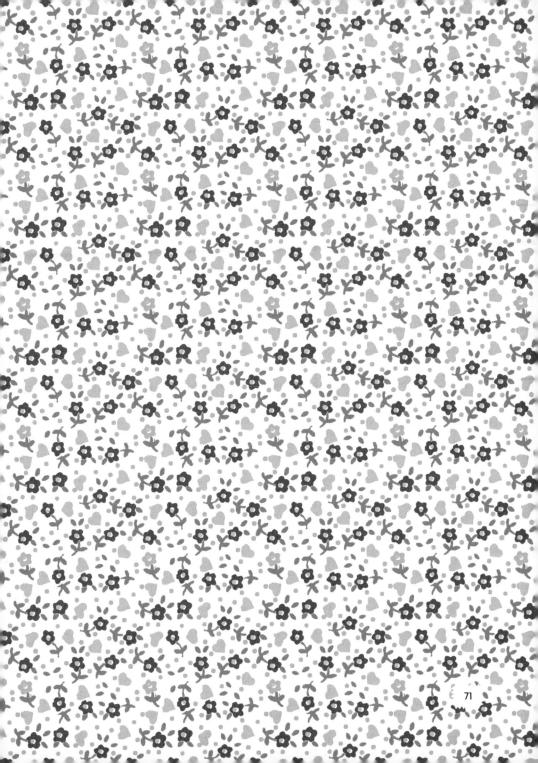

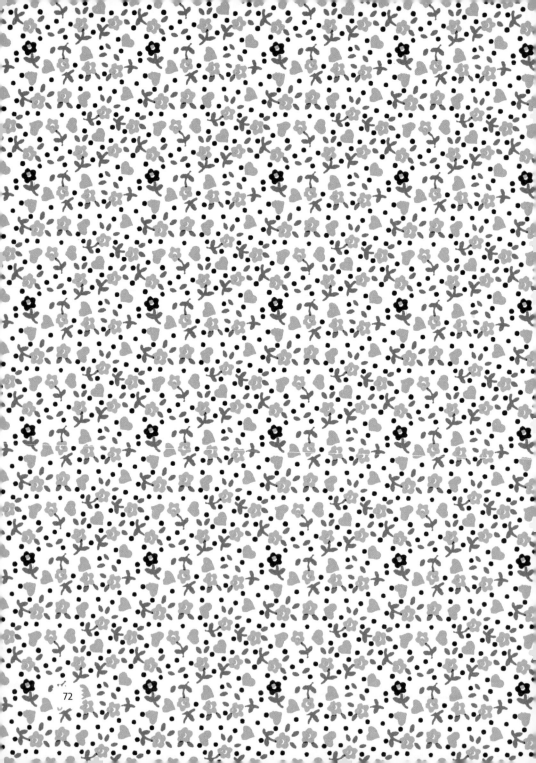

72

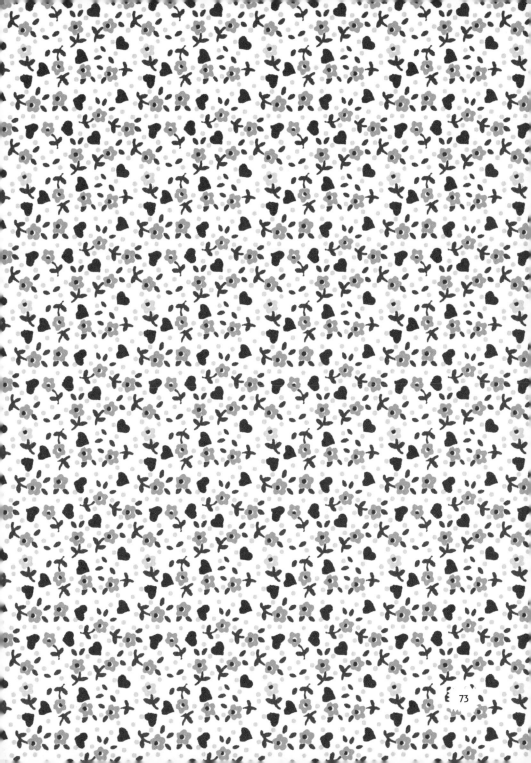

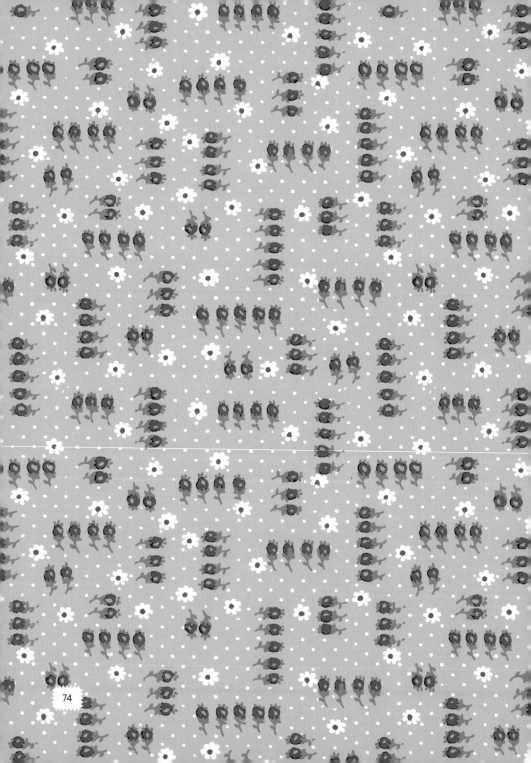

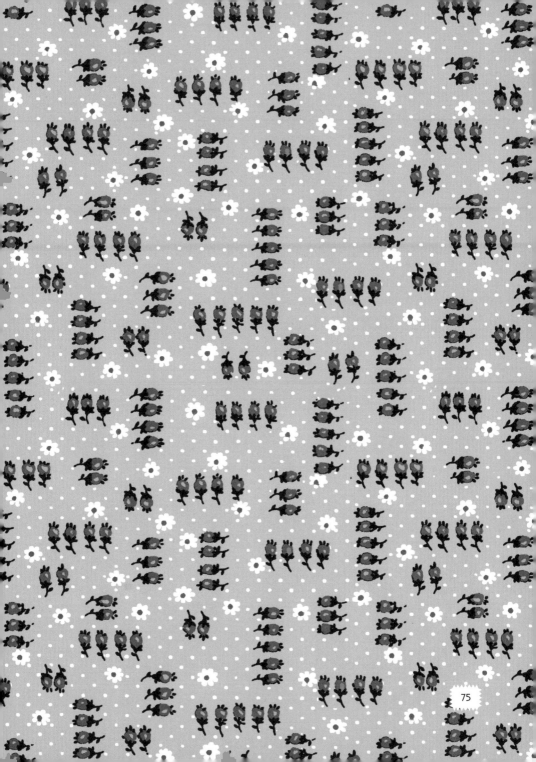

75

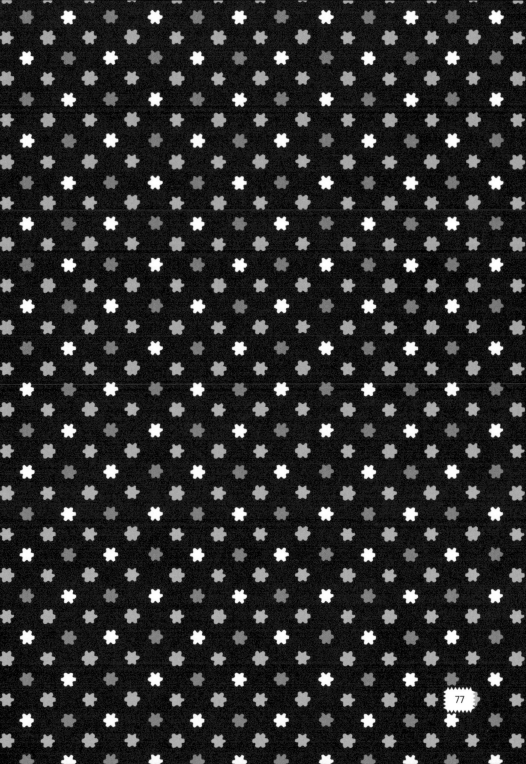

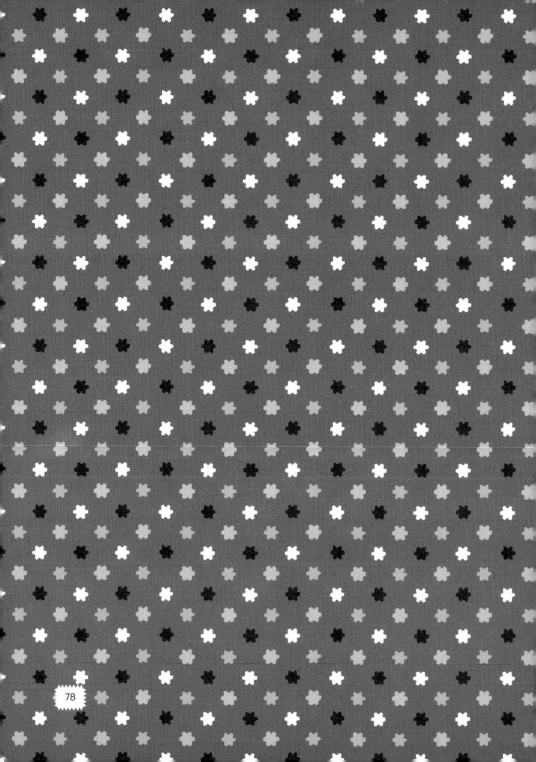

83

85

87

91

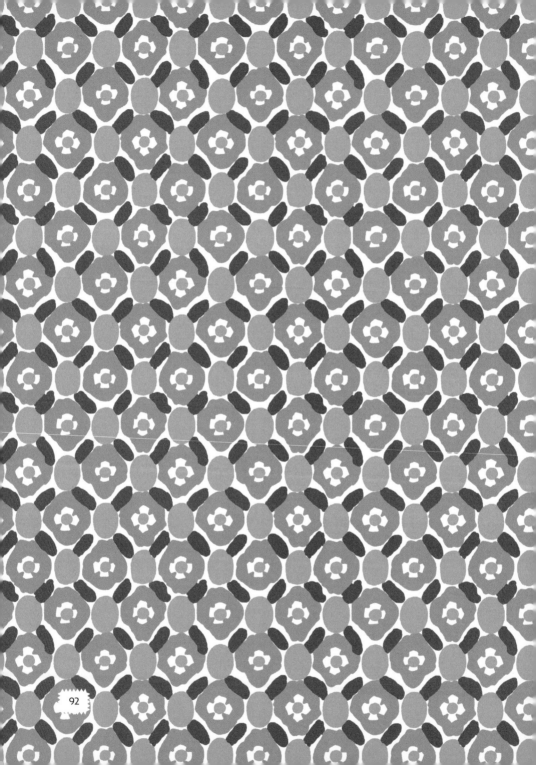

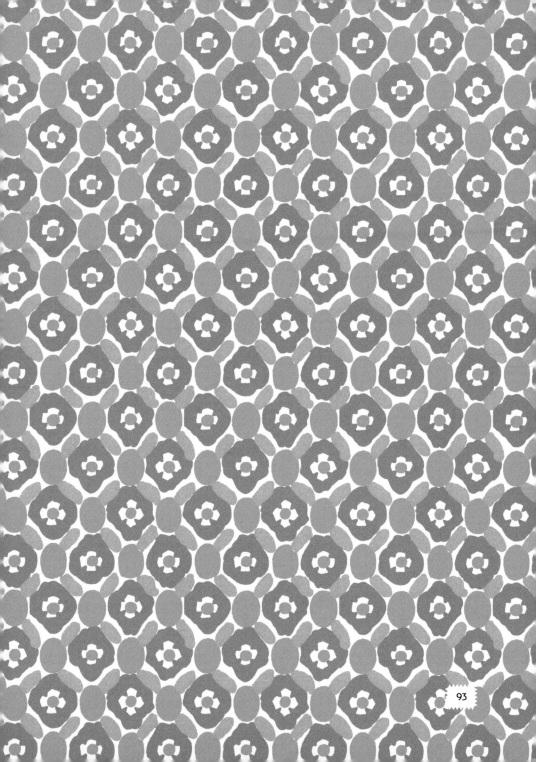

93

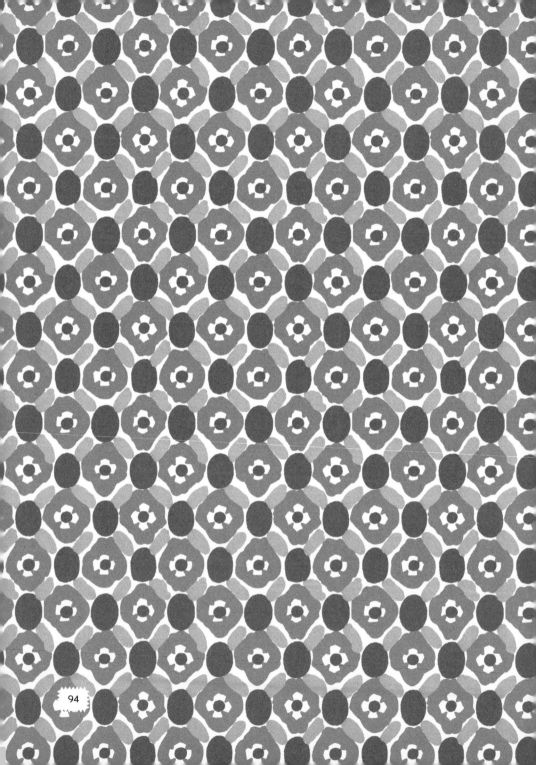

94

95

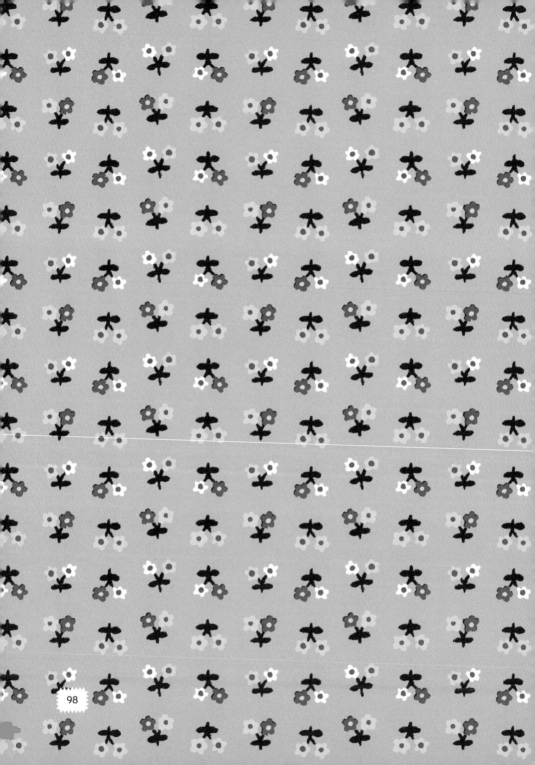

100

103

107

110

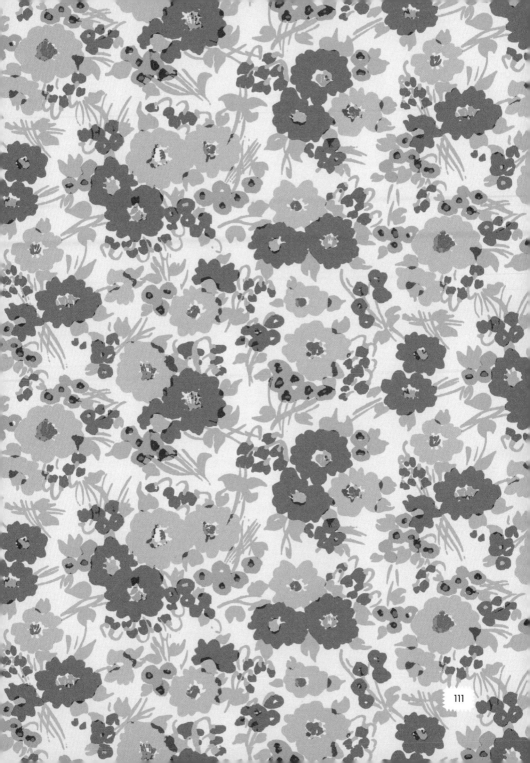

111

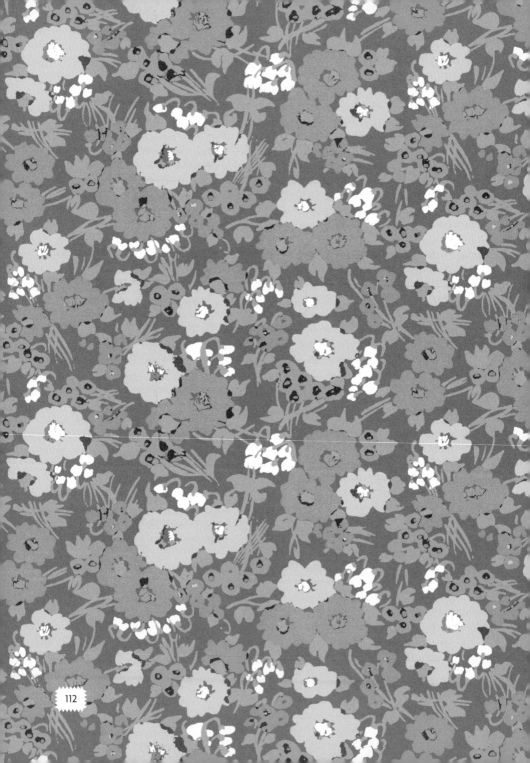

112

113

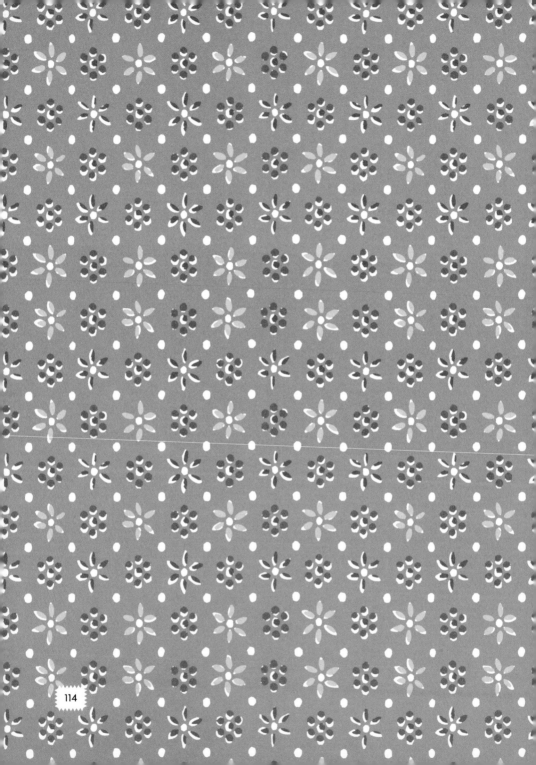

114

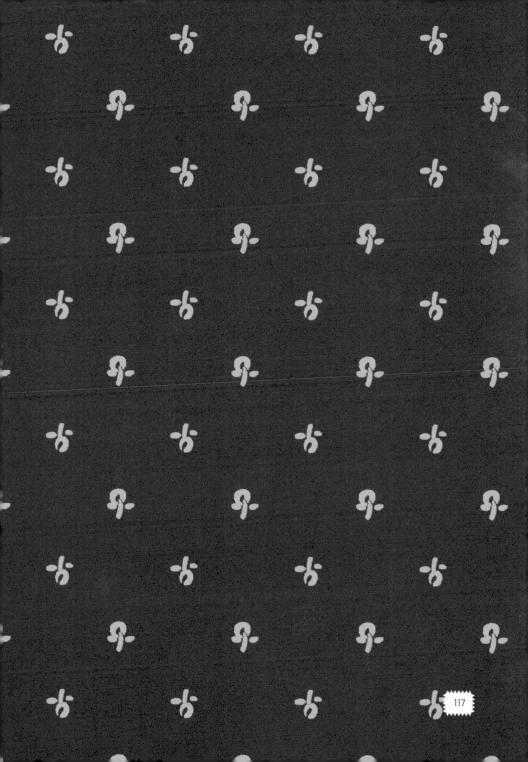

117

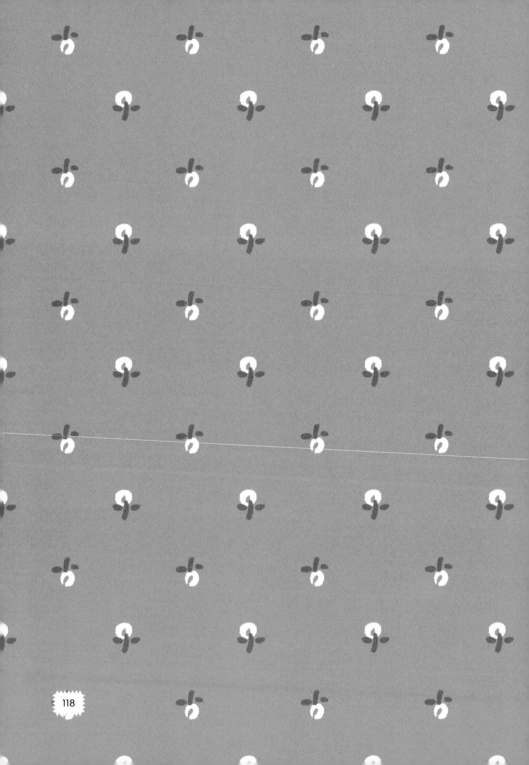

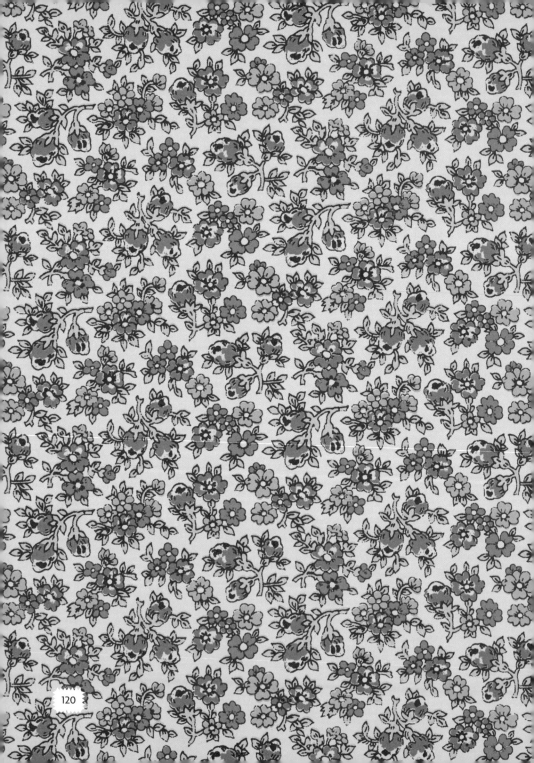

120

121

122

124

128

129

131

132

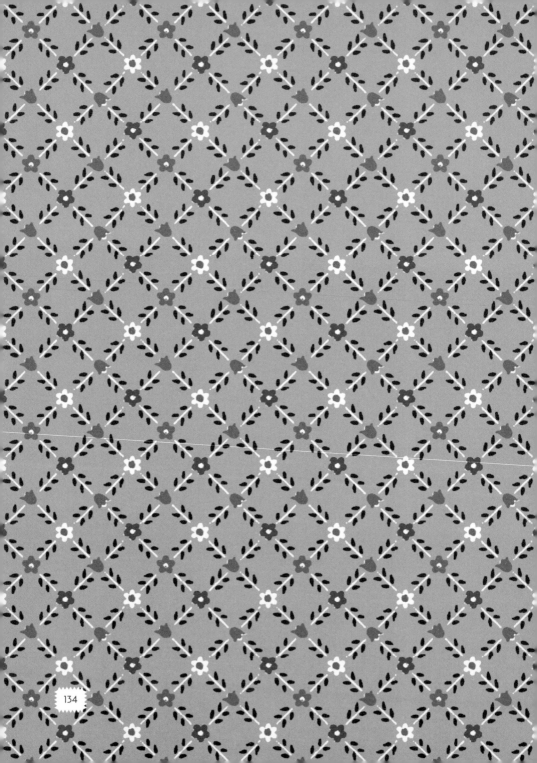

134

135

137

138

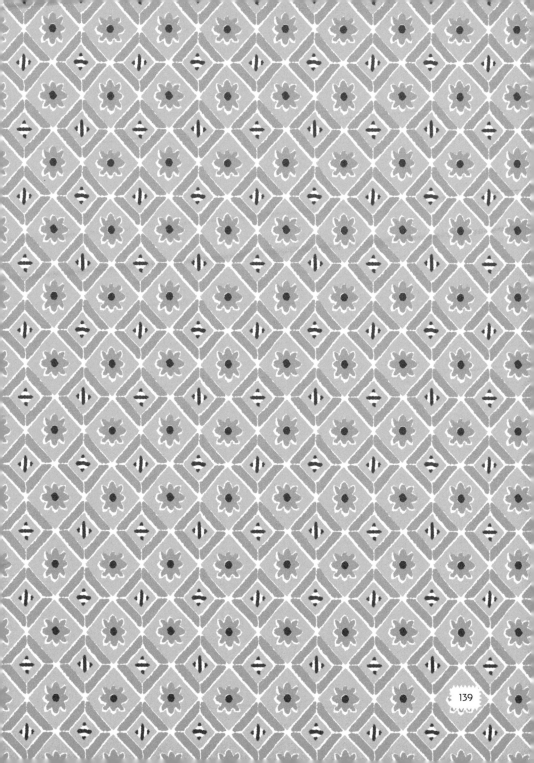

139

143

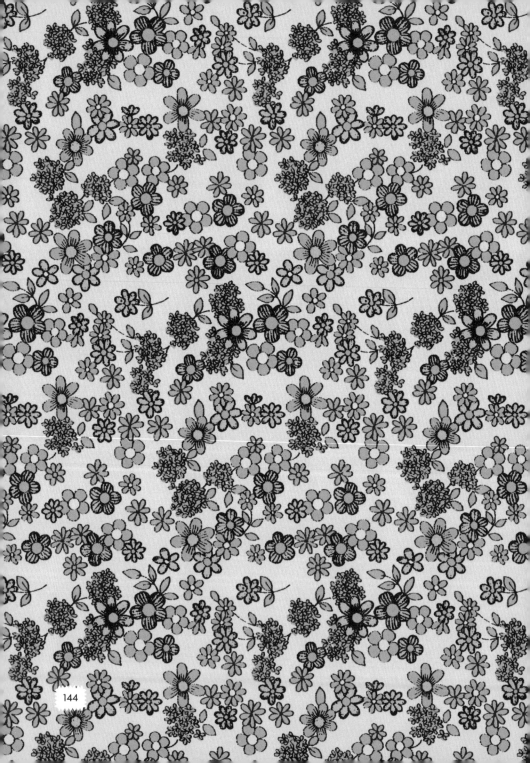

144

146

152

154

155

157

158

163

164

165

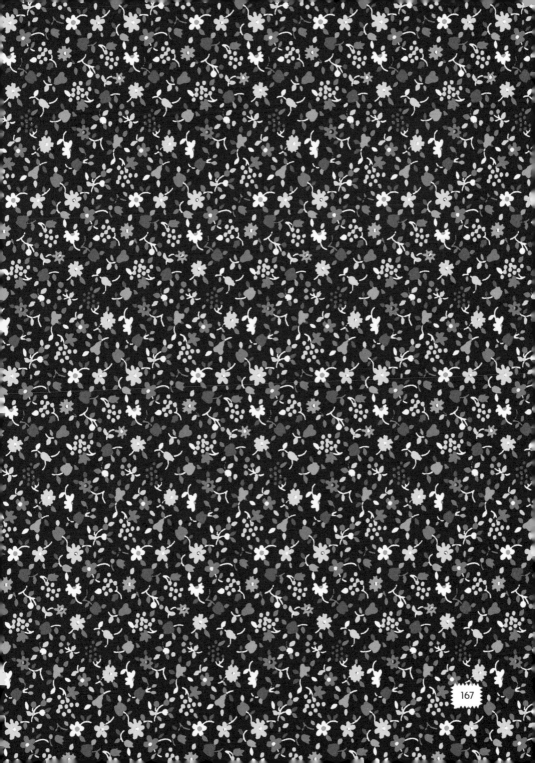

167

168

171

172

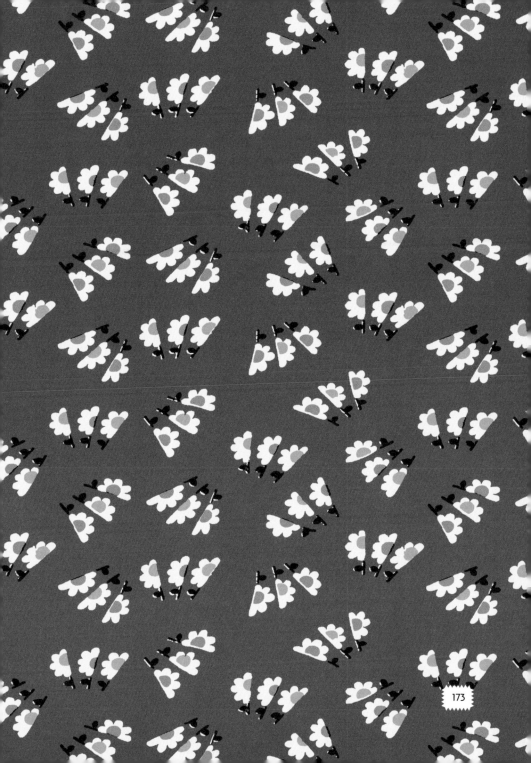

173

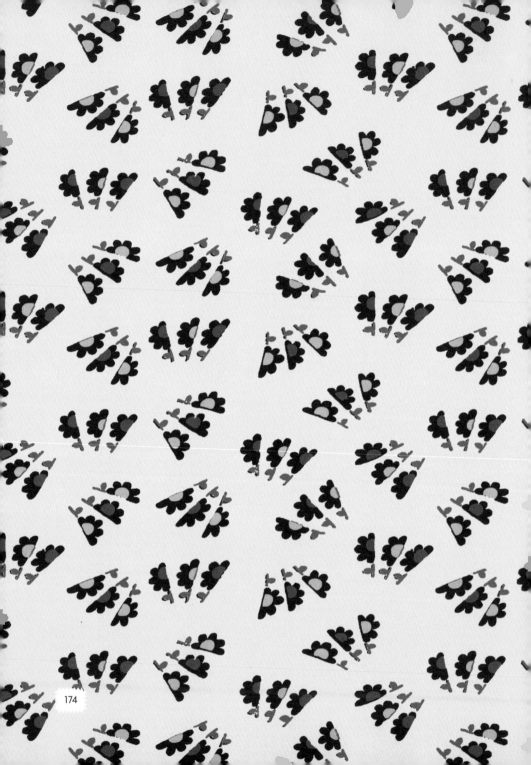

174

175

177

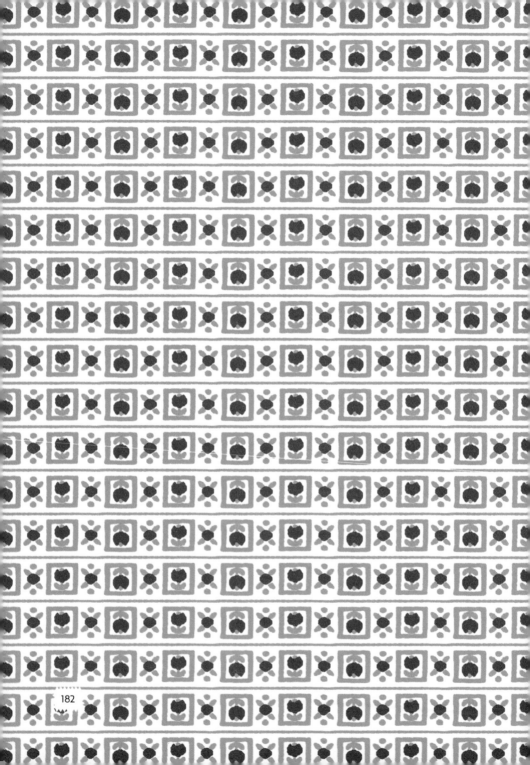

183

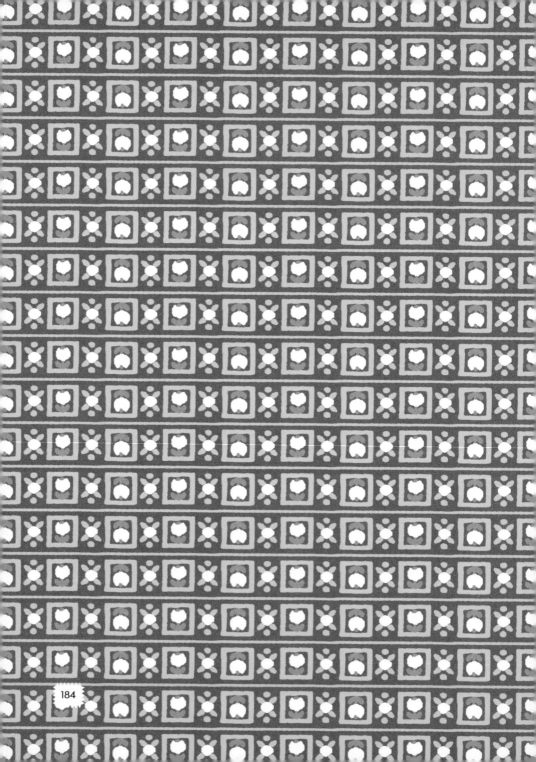

187

189

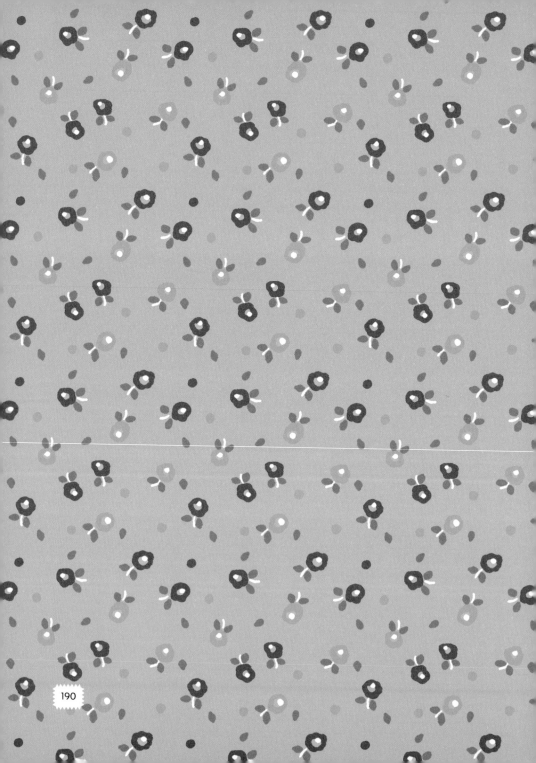

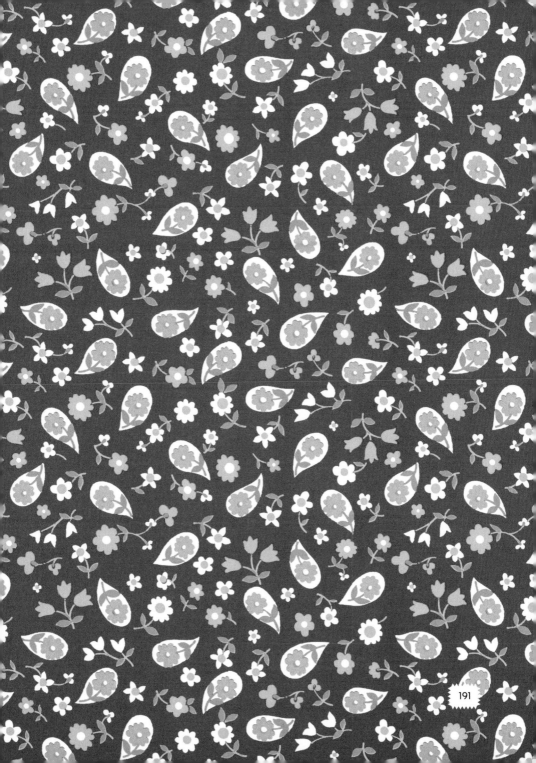

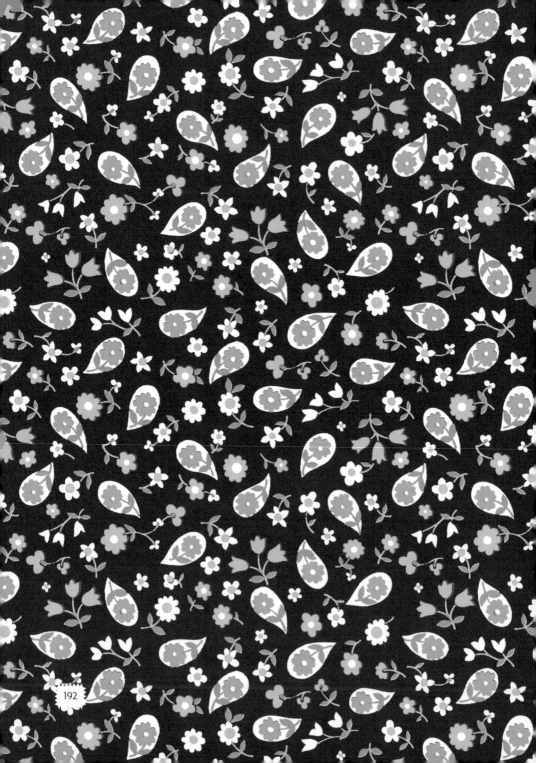

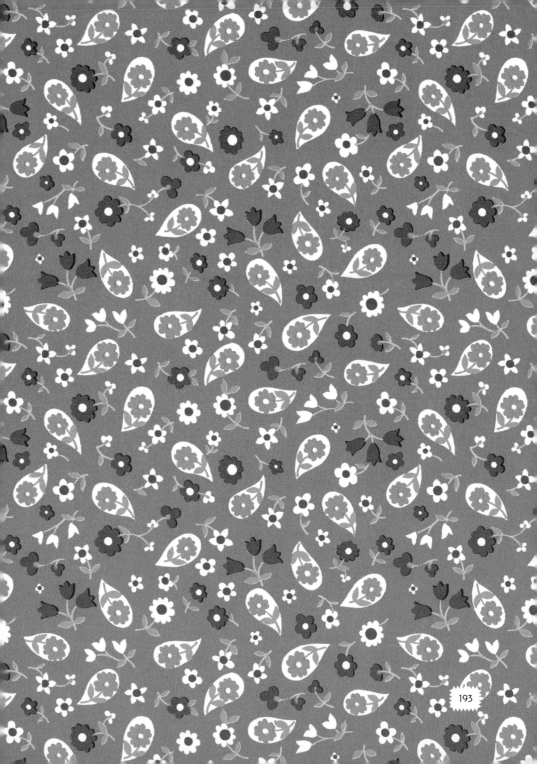

193

94

198

200

201

202

206

207

208

209

212

215

216

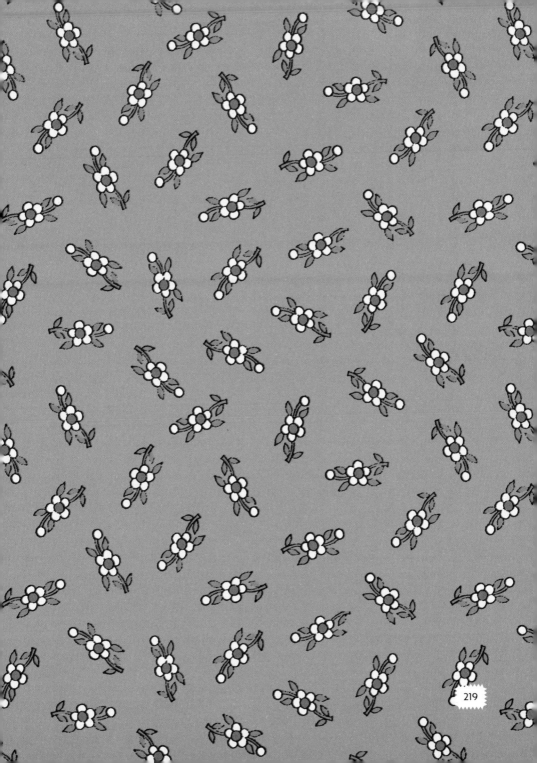

220

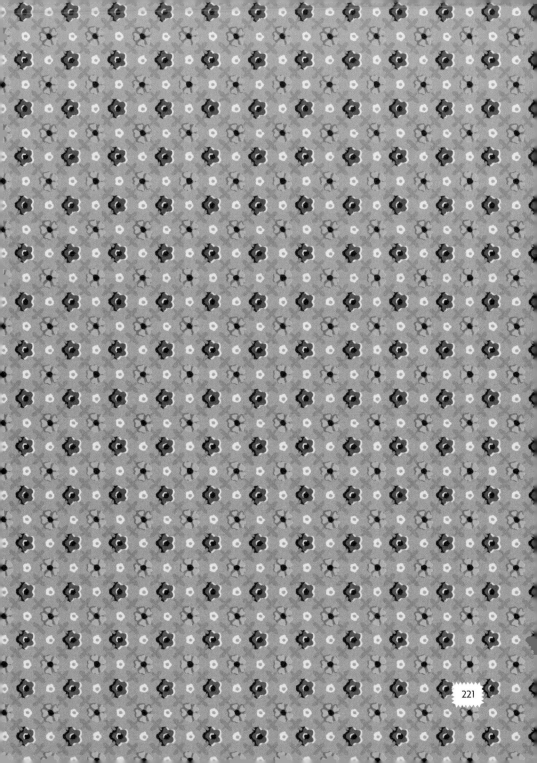

222

223

224

225

227

228

229

230

231

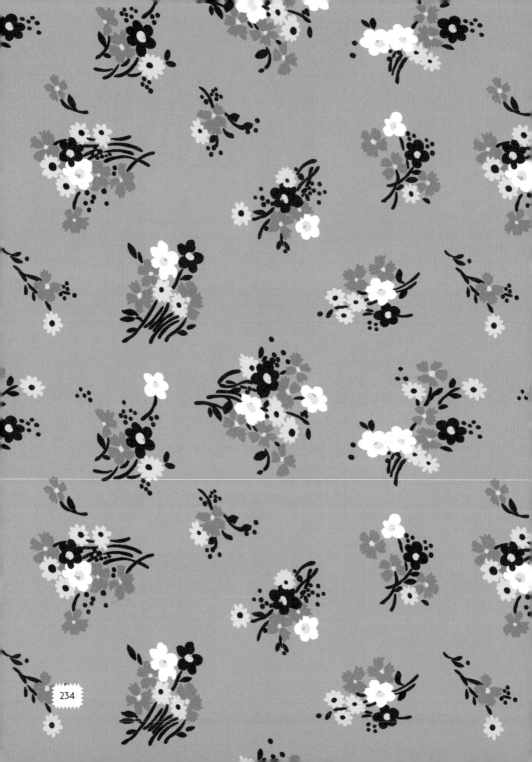

236

237

238

HOW TO USE THE DISK AND PATTERNS

Here are easy-to-follow instructions to help you use the pattern disk included with this book. If you're a new computer user, please do not be alarmed. You'll soon discover it's easy as pie (psst, probably easier) to access the patterns on the disk. In no time at all, you'll have at your fingertips the patterns you want to use. Or, if you're ultra-computer savvy, feel free to skip reading this section and drive solo!

I. WHAT IS INCLUDED ON THIS DISK?

- Textile patterns: Folder featuring Reprodepot's textile patterns in JPEG format
- Templates: Folder containing the templates you will need for the paper crafts

II. HOW DO I ACCESS THE DISK'S CONTENTS?

- Insert the disk into your computer. Click on the CD icon. You will see one folder, titled Reprodepot Patterns, that contains everything on the disk. Copy, or drag, the folder to your desktop.
- Now, open this folder from your desktop. The textile patterns are saved in JPEG format in the JPEG folder. JPEGs are compressed digital files that can be opened with several image-viewing programs, including either Photoshop or Illustrator.
- Simply use your pointer to browse

through the designs. You can preview and print the textile patterns from here. If you need to manipulate the patterns, see Steps III–V below.

- You can print the templates and/or resize them using Photoshop or Illustrator.

III. HOW DO I ENLARGE THE PATTERNS USING PHOTOSHOP?

- Once you've chosen a pattern, open its JPEG file in Photoshop and click on the Image Menu.
- Select "Image Size."
- Change the width of the image to 8.5" and make sure to constrain the proportions.
- Make sure the resolution is set at 300 pixels per inch.
- When resampling the image (an option at the bottom of this menu), I recommend changing "Bicubic" to "Bicubic Smoother."
- Crop the image to 8.5" x 11" by choosing the Crop Tool. Width and height boxes will appear under the menu bar. Enter 8.5 in the width box and 11 in the height box. (Your printer will probably not print all the way to the edge of the paper. It will automatically crop this image, so take that into consideration.)
- You can customize the size of the pattern if you have a printer that will allow for large-scale prints. Simply follow these steps and enter the preferred dimensions.

IV. HOW DO I TILE THE PATTERNS USING PHOTOSHOP?

- Open the JPEG pattern file in Photoshop.
- Now open a new document—the dimensions should be 11" x 8.5".
- Make sure the color mode is set to RGB and the print resolution is set to 300 pixels per inch.
- Use the Move Tool to drag your pattern into the new document. Align it to the left side of the new document.
- To repeat the pattern, copy and paste by selecting these options under the Edit Menu.
- Still using the Move Tool, adjust the images to match up, overlap, or sit side-by-side until you're satisfied with the repeat.
- As noted in Step III, your printer may crop this image.
- If printing with a printer that allows for large-scale prints, you can repeat these steps multiple times to make the image even bigger.

V. HOW DO I TILE THE PATTERNS USING ILLUSTRATOR?

- Open the JPEG pattern file in Illustrator.
- Under the File Menu, select "Document Setup."
- Change the page orientation to "Landscape" and click "OK."
- Use the Selection Tool to align the pattern to the left side of the document.

- To repeat the pattern, copy and paste by selecting these options under the Edit Menu.
- Still using the Selection Tool, adjust the images to match up, overlap or sit side-by-side until you're satisfied with the repeat.
- As noted in Step III, your printer may crop this image.
- If printing with a printer that allows for large-scale prints, you can repeat these steps multiple times to make the image even bigger.

EACH OF THESE SIMPLE AND HANDY PROJECTS REQUIRES A COLOR PRINTER, SCISSORS, AND 8 1/2" X 11" WHITE (PREFERABLY RECYCLED) TEXT-WEIGHT OR COVER-WEIGHT PAPER. ADDITIONAL MATERIALS NEEDED FOR SPECIFIC PROJECTS ARE LISTED WITH EACH PROJECT.

To help you get started, each project's difficulty level is indicated. Beginner crafters may want to start with "cinch" projects, such as the pretty and practical Tote Tag (page 245) or the Gift Wrap Medley (page 257). More seasoned crafters may opt to create an Anytime Flower Bouquet (page 251), unique Weave-Pattern Place Mats (page 261), or Party Invitation Suite (page 247), a gorgeous handmade invitation set including RSVP cards. Experts can dive right in with the Japanese-Inspired Stab-Bound Book (page 259) or the Accordion-Style Folder (page 263).

Whether a cinch or a challenge to complete, you can be sure that each craft project you choose to make will be well worth the time spent and become a beautiful, cherished item to keep or give.

TOTE TAG

MATERIALS NEEDED

tote tag template (on disk)

graph or ruled paper (see Note)

hole punch

reinforcements (you know, the white adhesive kind for punched holes)

felt or other pen

clear packing tape

ribbon or large rubber band

1. Print your textile pattern out on cover-weight paper. Then flip the sheet over and print the tote tag template on the blank side.

2. Pair this sheet up with the graph or ruled paper (if you're using ruled, make sure to position the paper so that the lines run parallel to the long side of the template), and cut through both sheets along the template lines. Use your hole punch to make the hole, and place a reinforcement over the hole on each sheet.

3. Write your contact info on the graph/ruled side, using your felt or other pen.

4. Match up the two paper pieces, back to back. "Laminate" the pieces together with clear packing tape. Trim the edges and repunch the hole.

5. Make a loop with your ribbon. Feed your looped ribbon or the rubber band through the hole and pull gently to secure.

6. Attach the tag to your bag or luggage. Bon voyage!

NOTE: If you would rather use your computer to print your contact info—great! Then you can use any paper you please.

PARTY INVITATION SUITE

MATERIALS NEEDED

handmade paper or card stock cut to 4½" x 6¼" and 3½" x 5" (one of each of these for each suite)

A6-size envelopes to match (your quantity plus one)

acid-free scrapbook adhesive or glue stick

bone folder

envelope template (on disk)

address label or circular seal sheets (available from your local office supply store)

BONUS! To make labels or seals, simply print your pattern on address label and circular seal sheets from the office supply store. You can run this through (as a background) and then print it out again with your address, monogram, or a motif.

1. Print or hand write your party invitation on the larger piece of card stock and your response card on the smaller piece.

2. To line the large outer envelope, make a template from the extra one. Open up and flatten the envelope, carefully cut around the inside edge of the adhesive and ¼" in from the bottom three edges. This solid piece is your template. Print your textile pattern on text-weight paper, then trace and cut out the lining. Use adhesive around the top edges to attach the lining to your envelopes, and use the bone folder to refold the envelope flap down.

3. To make the response card envelope, print your textile pattern out on text-weight paper. Then flip the sheet over and print the envelope template on the blank side. Cut precisely around the solid edges. Score along the dotted lines (you may want to use a straight edge), and fold in the flaps. Glue the bottom flap to the two side flaps. Then fold the top flap down to meet, using the tops of the side flaps as your guide. You will need to provide a seal for the response envelopes, as they are not gummed (see the bonus suggestion below!).

4. Now, cut a wrap or two to hold the envelope contents together. This could be as simple as a strip, cut lengthwise, wrapped around the middle and adhered. Or make two strips and layer them.

5. Assemble the suite. Place the response card and small envelope seal inside the small envelope. Slip the wrap over the invitation and response envelope and tuck inside the large envelope. Optionally, create a second seal for the large envelope.

PARTY DECORATIONS: PRETTY PAPER CHAIN, FLAG BANNER, DOT CURTAIN

MATERIALS NEEDED

paper trimmer (optional)

stapler

ribbon, string, or twine

glue stick

1" or larger hole punch

PRETTY PAPER CHAIN

Print your textile pattern(s) on both sides of cover-weight paper. Cut into strips (make any size you wish) using either a paper trimmer or scissors. Form one of the strips into a loop, grab your stapler, and staple the loop. Slide a strip through the first loop and staple to make a second link of the chain. Repeat. Repeat. Repeat. . . .

FLAG BANNER

Print a variety of patterns on text-weight paper. Cut these down to squares of any size you like. Fold the squares into triangles, opposite corners together. Slide the long edges over a long piece of ribbon, string, or twine to create a banner of the length desired. Secure the triangles to the ribbon with glue or staples, leaving one or two inches between the "flags" so the banner can hang gracefully.

DOT CURTAIN

Print a variety of patterns on cover-weight paper. Use the hole punch to punch out lots of dots. Adhere the dots at regular intervals to a long piece of ribbon, string, or twine by sandwiching the string between two glue stick–covered dots. Make several and hang from the ceiling or top of a window to create a whimsical curtain. This also makes a great garland.

ANYTIME FLOWER BOUQUET

MATERIALS NEEDED

small paint brush

green tempera paint

wooden chopsticks or skewers

a few sheets green construction paper

white glue

flower templates (on disk)

1" button

vase or wide satin ribbon for display

1. To make the stems, paint your chopsticks or skewers green and allow to dry. Cut free-form leaves from the construction paper and glue them to the stems.

2. To make the tulip, print your textile pattern on both sides of a sheet of cover-weight paper, and then run the paper through your printer once more to print out the tulip templates. Cut along the dotted line, and slide the two pieces together. Cut another small strip from your printed paper. Wrap and glue the strip to the top of a stem. Then, glue the covered stem to the tulip in the fold where the two pieces meet, aligning the edge of the strip with the bottom of the tulip.

3. To make the dandelion, print your textile pattern on both sides of a sheet of text-weight paper. Cut a strip 11" x 3". Cut notches three-quarters of the way accross the short side of the strip—for the entire length of the strip (it will resemble a chunky comb). Glue one end (just on the unnotched part) to the top of a stem and wind the strip around to form the flower. Then, adhere the second end with glue. Allow to dry thoroughly, then gently separate and push down the petal strips.

4. And finally, the daisy! Print your textile pattern on both sides of a sheet of cover-weight paper. Then run the paper through your printer two more times to print out the daisy template twice. Cut out both templates. Glue the two pieces together in the middle, rotating the shapes so that they do not match up. Trace around the button to make and cut out a 1" circle from the remaining tulip paper. Glue the circle in the middle of the top flower piece. To finish, simply glue one end of a stem to the back of the daisy.

5. Arrange your flowers in a vase or tie together with wide satin ribbon.

CHOOSE-A-DESIGN GREETING CARDS

MATERIALS NEEDED

blank card stock, cut into rectangles measuring 8½" x 5½" (cut one rectangle for each card you wish to make)

ruler

pencil

clear acrylic triangle with straight edge

bone folder

greeting card templates (on disk)

glue stick

hole punch (for the squirrel's eye)

felt pen

A1-size matching envelopes in your quantity

1. To score and fold your card, measure halfway, or 4¼" down the long end of your card stock and make a light pencil mark (you can erase it later). Align the short straight edge of the triangle with the bottom of the paper at the center mark. Run the point of your bone folder along the long end of the triangle (the center of your card). Now fold your card in half along the score line and crease with the edge of the bone folder. (You may eliminate this step by buying precut and scored cards at a craft supply store.)

2. Print out the greeting card template(s) on white text-weight paper. These templates are sized for A1-size cards (3½" x 5"). If you want to make larger or smaller shapes, adjust now with a photocopier. Once you have your templates sized, print your textile pattern on the other side of the sheet.

3. Carefully cut out your shape, and use the glue stick to adhere it to the front of the card. Use the hole punch to create the squirrel's eye before you glue it to the card. Play with the placement. Should it be centered? Or, set in the bottom right corner? Or, should you use two shapes, such as the dog and cat?

4. Write your greeting(s), assemble the cards and envelopes, and send or give to lucky family members and friends.

BONUS! Line the envelopes with a coordinating pattern (see Party Invitation Suite step 2, page 247). And, create labels or seals for the envelope (see Party Invitation Suite Bonus!, page 247).

DECORATIVE LIGHT-SWITCH COVER

MATERIALS NEEDED

light-switch cover

pencil

X-Acto knife

inexpensive small paint brush

decoupage glue

1. Print your textile pattern on text-weight paper. Then lay the light-switch cover face up on the blank side of the sheet. Trace around the inside and outside edges with the pencil. Cut out, leaving about a ½" border around the outer traced line. Notch the corners (outside the lines), to make folding easier. Use the X-Acto knife to cut out the inner rectangle along the lines.

2. Using the paint brush, cover the light-switch cover with glue. Working quickly and carefully, line up the paper and pat it down on the cover. Brush glue on the back sides of the paper flaps and fold them neatly to the back side of the cover, pressing out any wrinkles.

3. Allow your light-switch cover to dry, according to the glue's directions, and then reinstall on your wall. Don't worry about the screw holes. Simply feel around and poke through the paper with the screws when you reinstall.

GIFT WRAP MEDLEY

MATERIALS NEEDED

clear tape

ribbon or trim

pinking shears (optional)

mailing tube (optional)

1. Print a variety of textile patterns on text-weight paper. For larger packages, either neatly piece multiple sheets together (use clear tape on the inside seams) or take your print to the copy store and enlarge using a color photocopier.

2. Use this paper as you would any other wrapping paper.

3. Cut a long strip to make a band to place around a wrapped gift instead of a ribbon. Bust out your pinking shears, and pink the long edges of the band.

4. If you are gifting a print or poster, cover a mailing tube with your patterned paper.

5. For personalized cards, see Choose-a-Design Greeting Cards (page 253) as well as the instructions for constructing your own envelopes (see Party Invitation Suite step 3, page 247)—but use cover-weight paper and increase the size if necessary.

JAPANESE-INSPIRED STAB-BOUND BOOK

MATERIALS NEEDED

paper trimmer

text-weight paper for the pages of the book (cut to 5½" x 8½")

3 spring clamps

book hole template (on disk)

hole punch

pencil

electric drill with ⅛" bit, or an awl (and a piece of wood or board to place under paper while drilling)

large embroidery or bookbinding needle

bookbinding thread—or substitute embroidery thread, yarn, dental floss, or string

white glue

1. The finished book will measure 5½" x 8½". To make the cover and end pages, print one textile pattern on two sheets of cover-weight paper, then flip the sheets over and print another design on the other sides. Cut each piece into rectangles measuring 5½" x 8½".

2. Assemble the book, precisely sandwiching the text paper between the printed pieces. Hold this assemblage together with a spring clamp on each of the two short sides and one on the long side.

3. Print out the book hole template on scrap paper. Cut along the lines and punch out the holes. Place the template on the free edge of your book. Use your pencil to mark where you'll drill the holes.

4. Carefully drill the holes or use an awl to make them.

5. Bind the book using the drilled holes as a stitch guide. With your needle threaded, begin sewing from the back of the book to the front, leaving a little tail. Wrap the thread around the top edge and then lace it through the same hole again. Then bring it around the side edge and push through the same hole once again (see Illustration). Work down the length of the book, alternating front and back sides. At each hole, encircle the side edge again. When you reach the bottom of the book, work straight back up in the opposite direction until you reach the first hole and the tail. Tie off your thread and trim. For added security, glue the little ends of thread down.

SAFETY NOTE: Children will enjoy making this project but adults only should operate the drill, and younger children should be closely supervised if using an awl.

WEAVE-PATTERN PLACE MATS

MATERIALS NEEDED

paper trimmer

clear tape

clear contact paper or a laminator

1. The finished place mats will measure 11" x 17". Print a variety of textile patterns on text-weight paper.

2. Cut the printed paper into 1" strips. Carefully tape two like strips together, intersecting the two short ends to create a seam with no overlap. For each place mat, trim 17 of the long strips you just made to 11" and 11 of the strips to 17".

3. Now weave! Use your creativity and love of vintage textile designs to guide your pattern. Start by laying out one 17" strip. Then, alternating front, back, front, back, etc., tape (on the backside only, and just enough to secure the strip) the short strips to the bottom (see Illustration). Keep alternating and weave the rest of the long strips through. Tape where needed but remember, these will be laminated. Try creating stripes or plaids. Or, go monochromatic or use only two colors.

4. To finish the place mats, cover both sides with clear contact paper and trim, leaving about a ¼" clear border (I always like to round the corners). Or, take your finished weavings to your local copy shop and use a self-serve laminator.

ACCORDION-STYLE FOLDER

MATERIALS NEEDED

18" x 24" sheet of colored heavy-weight drawing paper (from the art supply store)

yardstick

pencil

bone folder

acid-free scrapbook adhesive or glue stick

1. Print your textile pattern out on two sheets of cover-weight paper. Then cut both sheets to 6½" x 11" (see Note).

2. Place your drawing paper, horizontal orientation, on a flat surface. Using diagram A as your guide, draw the following lines: measure 9" down, draw a horizontal line center; make 9 lines total, 4 on each side of the center line ½" apart. Use your bone folder and yardstick to score every line. Then, draw and score two vertical lines 6½" in from each side. Cut out 6½" square corners (dotted lines on the diagram). Cut little notches to meet the lines, as shown.

3. To make the accordion pleats, fold the paper in half bottom-to-top with the pencil lines facing out. Following your scoring, fold back and forth at each line (diagram B).

4. Make diagonal folds in the pleats—this step is important. Mitre the corners and fold the pleated arms up to the sides of the front and back, making a deep crease (diagram C).

5. Open up your paper, and fold the arms up. Recrease everything and follow the diagonal creases that you just made. Glue the notched flaps to the body of the folder (diagram D).

6. To finish, glue the two patterned cover pieces to the front and back of the folder.

7. Now fill your folder with those business receipts you've been intending to enter into QuickBooks or your collection of Christian Bale magazine clippings. . .

NOTE: If your printer will not print an area this long, simply adhere two 6½" x 5½" pieces together.

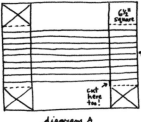

diagram A

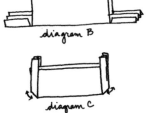

diagram B

diagram C

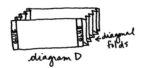

diagram D

LICENSE AGREEMENT

Reprodepot's Pattern Book: Flora ("The Swatches") on this disk ("The Disk") are licensed for use under the following Terms and Conditions, which define what You may do with the product. Please read them carefully. Use of The Swatches on The Disk implies that You have read and accepted these terms and conditions in full. If You do not agree to the terms and conditions of this agreement, do not use or copy The Swatches. If you reject the terms of this Agreement within thirty (30) days after purchasing this product, you may call Chronicle Books at (415) 537-4200 to request a full refund of the purchase price.

TERMS AND CONDITIONS OF USE

You have agreed to use The Swatches under the following Terms and Conditions:

AGREEMENT

These Terms and Conditions constitute a legal Agreement between the purchaser ("You" or "Your") and Reprodepot, Inc.

LICENSE

The Swatches on the Disk are owned by Reprodepot and are licensed, not sold, to You for use pursuant to the terms of this Agreement. You have a nonexclusive, nontransferable, nonsublicensable license to use, modify, reproduce, publish, and display The Swatches provided that You comply with the Terms and Conditions of this Agreement. The Swatches are protected by the copyright laws of the United States.

You may permanently transfer all of your rights and obligations under the License Agreement to another by physically transferring the original media (e.g., the CD-ROM and book you purchased) and all original packaging; provided, however, that you permanently delete all copies and installations of The Swatches in your possession or control, and that the recipient agrees to the terms of this License Agreement. The transferor (i.e., You), and not Reprodepot, agrees to be solely responsible for any taxes, fees, charges, duties, withholdings, assessments, and the like, together with any interest, penalties, and additions imposed in connection with such transfer.

PERMITTED USES

The Swatches are intended for use in personal projects. You may, subject to the Terms and Conditions of this Agreement, for example:
1. Print The Swatches in any of the provided formats and incorporate into personal projects.
2. Use one copy of The Disk on a single workstation or computer only.
3. Backup The Swatches to one hard drive.
4. Tile or crop The Swatches.
5. Display The Swatches on, or incorporate into the design of, a personal web site at a resolution of 72dpi.
6. Use The Swatches as background wallpaper in personal video projects.
7. Print The Swatches to make small runs of up to 10 copies of an item produced by an individual artist or craftsperson that incorporates a Swatch, provided that the retail value of each item does not exceed $100.

RESTRICTIONS

You may not:
1. Make any commercial use of The Swatches not expressly listed in Permitted Uses. If you wish to make commercial use of The Swatches that exceeds the scope of this license, please contact licensing@reprodepot.com.
2. Distribute, copy, transfer, assign, rent, lease, resell, give away, or barter The Swatches, electronically or in hard copy, except as expressly permitted under the Permitted Uses above.
3. Post The Swatches online in a downloadable format.

4. Distribute or incorporate The Swatches into another template library or any similar product, or otherwise make available The Swatches for use or distribution separately or detached from this product.

5. Modify and use The Swatches in connection with pornographic, libelous, obscene, immoral, defamatory, or otherwise illegal material.

6. Transfer possession of The Swatches to another person either across a network, on a CD, or by any other method now known or hereafter invented.

7. Digitally modify or manipulate The Swatches.

8. Change the scale or color of The Swatches.

9. Electronically extract elements of The Swatches.

TERMINATION

1. By using The Swatches, you agree that The Swatches are works of art subject to protection under the United States Copyright Act, 17 U.S.C. 101 et seq. Penalties for copyright infringement can include statutory damages of $750 to $30,000 per infringement, or up to $150,000 in the case of willful infringement. The prevailing party may also be entitled to recover attorney's fees.

2. This license is in force until terminated. If You do not comply with the terms and conditions above, the license automatically terminates. At termination, You must immediately (i) stop using The Swatches, (ii) destroy The Swatches or, at the request of Reprodepot, return the product to Reprodepot, and (iii) delete or remove The Swatches from Your premises, computer systems, and electronic or physical storage. Should Reprodepot or Chronicle Books incur any attorney fees or other costs in collecting or enforcing this License, You agree to reimburse Reprodepot and Chronicle Books for all such fees and costs.

WARRANTIES

1. Chronicle Books warrants that the media on which The Swatches are supplied will be free from defects in material and workmanship under normal use for 90 days. Any media found to be defective will be replaced free of charge by returning the media to Chronicle Books with a copy of Your receipt.

2. The Swatches are provided "as is," "as available," and "with all faults," without warranty of any kind, either expressed or implied, including but not limited to the implied warranties or merchantability and fitness for a particular purpose. The entire risk as to quality, accuracy, and performance of The Swatches is with You. In no event will Reprodepot or Chronicle Books, their employees, directors, officers, or agents or dealers, or anyone else associated with Reprodepot or Chronicle Books be liable to You for any damages, including any lost profit, lost savings, or any other consequential damages arising from the use of or inability to use The Swatches even if Reprodepot or Chronicle Books, their employees, directors, officers, or agents or authorized dealers, or anyone else associated with Reprodepot or Chronicle Books has been advised of the possibility of such damages or for any claim by any other party. Our maximum liability to You shall not exceed the amount paid for the product.

3. Your use of The Swatches will not violate any applicable law or regulation of any country, state, or other governmental entity.

4. You warrant that You will not use The Swatches in any way that is not permitted by this Agreement.

5. You agree to indemnify and hold Reprodepot and Chronicle Books harmless against all claims arising out of any breach of this Agreement.

GENERAL

You acknowledge that You have read this agreement, understand it, and agree to be bound by its terms and conditions. You further agree that it supersedes any proposal or prior agreement, oral or written, and that it may not be changed except by a signed written agreement.

THUMBNAIL INDEX

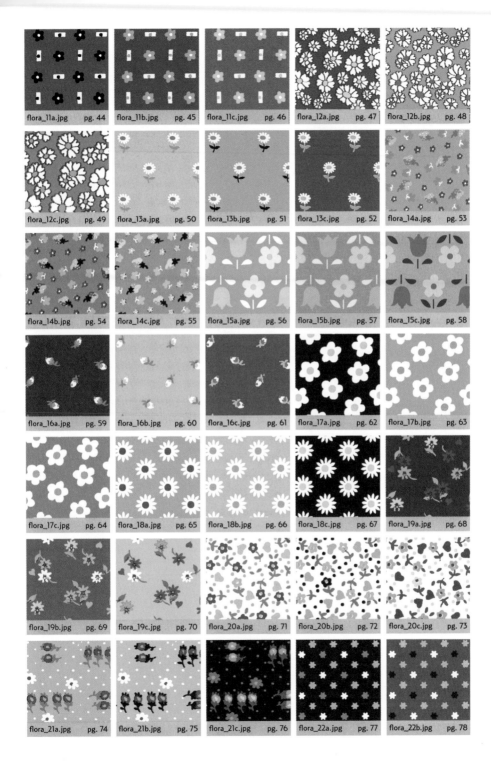

flora_11a.jpg   pg. 44
flora_11b.jpg   pg. 45
flora_11c.jpg   pg. 46
flora_12a.jpg   pg. 47
flora_12b.jpg   pg. 48

flora_12c.jpg   pg. 49
flora_13a.jpg   pg. 50
flora_13b.jpg   pg. 51
flora_13c.jpg   pg. 52
flora_14a.jpg   pg. 53

flora_14b.jpg   pg. 54
flora_14c.jpg   pg. 55
flora_15a.jpg   pg. 56
flora_15b.jpg   pg. 57
flora_15c.jpg   pg. 58

flora_16a.jpg   pg. 59
flora_16b.jpg   pg. 60
flora_16c.jpg   pg. 61
flora_17a.jpg   pg. 62
flora_17b.jpg   pg. 63

flora_17c.jpg   pg. 64
flora_18a.jpg   pg. 65
flora_18b.jpg   pg. 66
flora_18c.jpg   pg. 67
flora_19a.jpg   pg. 68

flora_19b.jpg   pg. 69
flora_19c.jpg   pg. 70
flora_20a.jpg   pg. 71
flora_20b.jpg   pg. 72
flora_20c.jpg   pg. 73

flora_21a.jpg   pg. 74
flora_21b.jpg   pg. 75
flora_21c.jpg   pg. 76
flora_22a.jpg   pg. 77
flora_22b.jpg   pg. 78

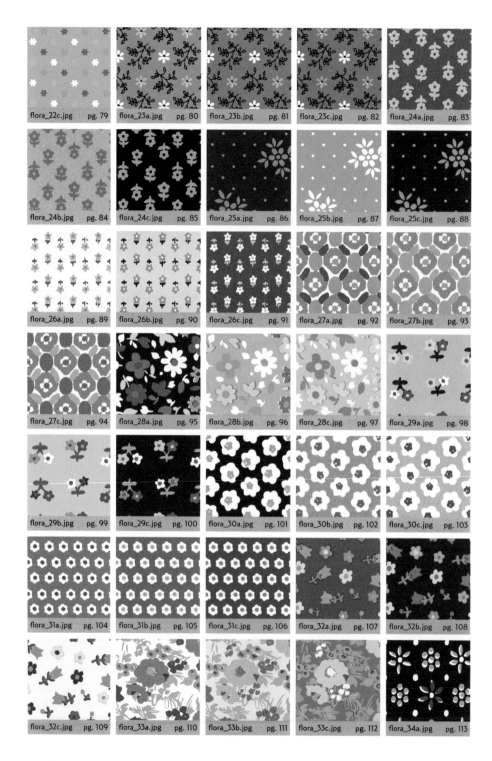

flora_22c.jpg   pg. 79
flora_23a.jpg   pg. 80
flora_23b.jpg   pg. 81
flora_23c.jpg   pg. 82
flora_24a.jpg   pg. 83

flora_24b.jpg   pg. 84
flora_24c.jpg   pg. 85
flora_25a.jpg   pg. 86
flora_25b.jpg   pg. 87
flora_25c.jpg   pg. 88

flora_26a.jpg   pg. 89
flora_26b.jpg   pg. 90
flora_26c.jpg   pg. 91
flora_27a.jpg   pg. 92
flora_27b.jpg   pg. 93

flora_27c.jpg   pg. 94
flora_28a.jpg   pg. 95
flora_28b.jpg   pg. 96
flora_28c.jpg   pg. 97
flora_29a.jpg   pg. 98

flora_29b.jpg   pg. 99
flora_29c.jpg   pg. 100
flora_30a.jpg   pg. 101
flora_30b.jpg   pg. 102
flora_30c.jpg   pg. 103

flora_31a.jpg   pg. 104
flora_31b.jpg   pg. 105
flora_31c.jpg   pg. 106
flora_32a.jpg   pg. 107
flora_32b.jpg   pg. 108

flora_32c.jpg   pg. 109
flora_33a.jpg   pg. 110
flora_33b.jpg   pg. 111
flora_33c.jpg   pg. 112
flora_34a.jpg   pg. 113

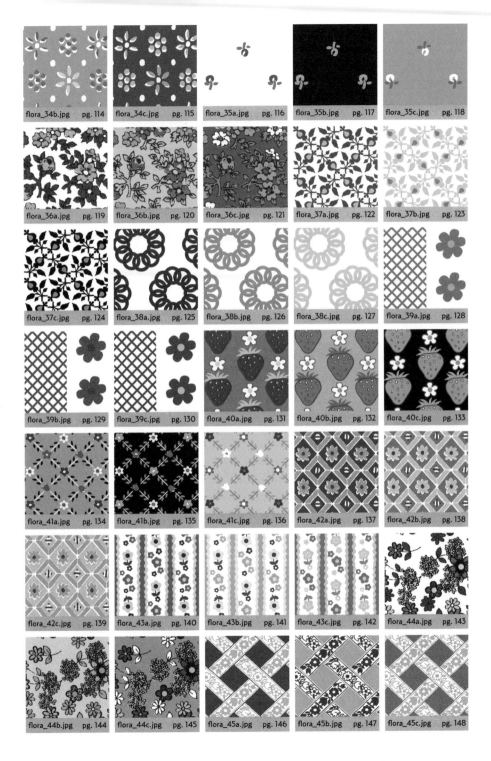

flora_34b.jpg   pg. 114

flora_34c.jpg   pg. 115

flora_35a.jpg   pg. 116

flora_35b.jpg   pg. 117

flora_35c.jpg   pg. 118

flora_36a.jpg   pg. 119

flora_36b.jpg   pg. 120

flora_36c.jpg   pg. 121

flora_37a.jpg   pg. 122

flora_37b.jpg   pg. 123

flora_37c.jpg   pg. 124

flora_38a.jpg   pg. 125

flora_38b.jpg   pg. 126

flora_38c.jpg   pg. 127

flora_39a.jpg   pg. 128

flora_39b.jpg   pg. 129

flora_39c.jpg   pg. 130

flora_40a.jpg   pg. 131

flora_40b.jpg   pg. 132

flora_40c.jpg   pg. 133

flora_41a.jpg   pg. 134

flora_41b.jpg   pg. 135

flora_41c.jpg   pg. 136

flora_42a.jpg   pg. 137

flora_42b.jpg   pg. 138

flora_42c.jpg   pg. 139

flora_43a.jpg   pg. 140

flora_43b.jpg   pg. 141

flora_43c.jpg   pg. 142

flora_44a.jpg   pg. 143

flora_44b.jpg   pg. 144

flora_44c.jpg   pg. 145

flora_45a.jpg   pg. 146

flora_45b.jpg   pg. 147

flora_45c.jpg   pg. 148

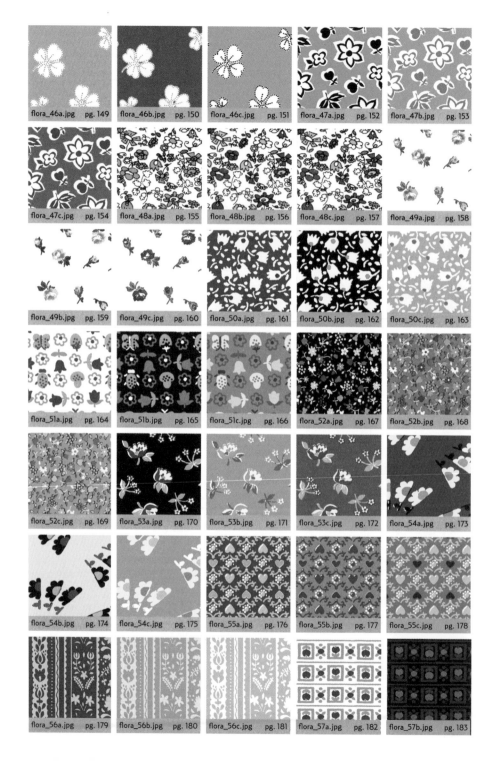

flora_46a.jpg   pg. 149
flora_46b.jpg   pg. 150
flora_46c.jpg   pg. 151
flora_47a.jpg   pg. 152
flora_47b.jpg   pg. 153

flora_47c.jpg   pg. 154
flora_48a.jpg   pg. 155
flora_48b.jpg   pg. 156
flora_48c.jpg   pg. 157
flora_49a.jpg   pg. 158

flora_49b.jpg   pg. 159
flora_49c.jpg   pg. 160
flora_50a.jpg   pg. 161
flora_50b.jpg   pg. 162
flora_50c.jpg   pg. 163

flora_51a.jpg   pg. 164
flora_51b.jpg   pg. 165
flora_51c.jpg   pg. 166
flora_52a.jpg   pg. 167
flora_52b.jpg   pg. 168

flora_52c.jpg   pg. 169
flora_53a.jpg   pg. 170
flora_53b.jpg   pg. 171
flora_53c.jpg   pg. 172
flora_54a.jpg   pg. 173

flora_54b.jpg   pg. 174
flora_54c.jpg   pg. 175
flora_55a.jpg   pg. 176
flora_55b.jpg   pg. 177
flora_55c.jpg   pg. 178

flora_56a.jpg   pg. 179
flora_56b.jpg   pg. 180
flora_56c.jpg   pg. 181
flora_57a.jpg   pg. 182
flora_57b.jpg   pg. 183

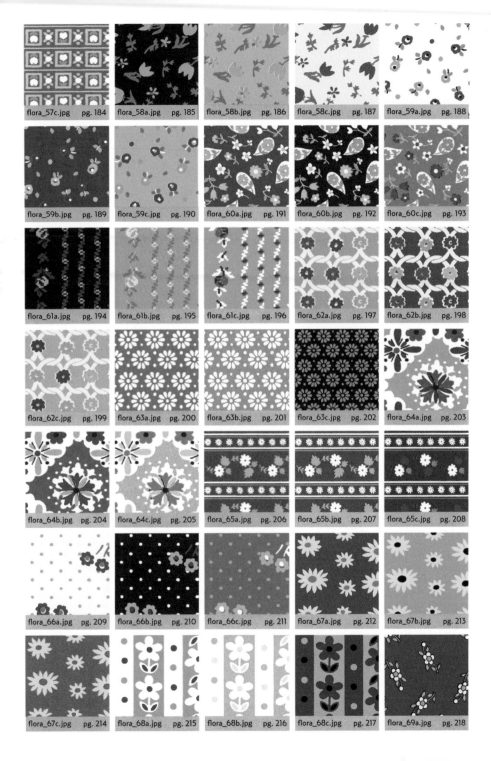

flora_57c.jpg   pg. 184
flora_58a.jpg   pg. 185
flora_58b.jpg   pg. 186
flora_58c.jpg   pg. 187
flora_59a.jpg   pg. 188

flora_59b.jpg   pg. 189
flora_59c.jpg   pg. 190
flora_60a.jpg   pg. 191
flora_60b.jpg   pg. 192
flora_60c.jpg   pg. 193

flora_61a.jpg   pg. 194
flora_61b.jpg   pg. 195
flora_61c.jpg   pg. 196
flora_62a.jpg   pg. 197
flora_62b.jpg   pg. 198

flora_62c.jpg   pg. 199
flora_63a.jpg   pg. 200
flora_63b.jpg   pg. 201
flora_63c.jpg   pg. 202
flora_64a.jpg   pg. 203

flora_64b.jpg   pg. 204
flora_64c.jpg   pg. 205
flora_65a.jpg   pg. 206
flora_65b.jpg   pg. 207
flora_65c.jpg   pg. 208

flora_66a.jpg   pg. 209
flora_66b.jpg   pg. 210
flora_66c.jpg   pg. 211
flora_67a.jpg   pg. 212
flora_67b.jpg   pg. 213

flora_67c.jpg   pg. 214
flora_68a.jpg   pg. 215
flora_68b.jpg   pg. 216
flora_68c.jpg   pg. 217
flora_69a.jpg   pg. 218

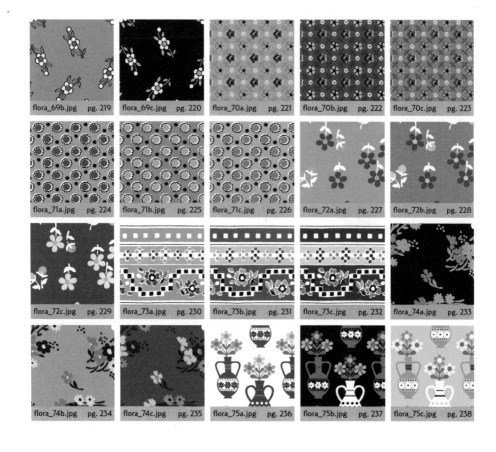

flora_69b.jpg   pg. 219
flora_69c.jpg   pg. 220
flora_70a.jpg   pg. 221
flora_70b.jpg   pg. 222
flora_70c.jpg   pg. 223

flora_71a.jpg   pg. 224
flora_71b.jpg   pg. 225
flora_71c.jpg   pg. 226
flora_72a.jpg   pg. 227
flora_72b.jpg   pg. 228

flora_72c.jpg   pg. 229
flora_73a.jpg   pg. 230
flora_73b.jpg   pg. 231
flora_73c.jpg   pg. 232
flora_74a.jpg   pg. 233

flora_74b.jpg   pg. 234
flora_74c.jpg   pg. 235
flora_75a.jpg   pg. 236
flora_75b.jpg   pg. 237
flora_75c.jpg   pg. 238